Beautiful Coincidence

Stephanie Wert

BookLeaf Publishing

India | USA | UK

Made with ❤ on the BookLeaf Publishing Platform
www.bookleafpub.in
www.bookleafpub.com

Dedication

It is my blessing to dedicate this book to Mahmoud and Lena, as well as every Palestinian and resilient soul existing. You taught me love amidst your own suffering, trust when the world betrayed its humanity and grace for our human imperfections. It will always fill my heart to be called family by you.

Preface

This book of poems is my ode to the Palestinian resistance that lives in each smile.

Acknowledgements

I would like to acknowledge the light in me which is able to shine by Gods grace. May anyone who reads this journey be able to grow through my pain and see the candle still burning in the end.

My soul has returned

My soul has returned
So you can live
To share our purpose
Of hope and love
Sent down through prayers
Shown through light
Racing through the veins of paradise
Mixing with the soul of the sea
The heartbeat remains
All will return
Heavenly keys unlock new beginnings
The sky and birds protect the innocent
For you child of Gaza
Are an angel
I pass my love to you
So my soul can return
To the one above

The tree and the seed

In a land untouched by man there stood a grand oak tree
and a little seed
This oak some say was aged as far back as Adam and
Eve
His trunk stood sturdy and solid like the Earth
He took great pride to raise this small seed from birth
God told him watch and follow my commands
for you will raise this seed better than man
The tree agreed and patiently he waited
but for how long could he wait on Gods plan
Using his branches for cover during the hot summers
This seed would not budge despite the food and water
What else did God want him to offer
Growing inpatient he yelled at the seed
Why are you doing this to me!
Lightning struck the oak tree split in half
This was God speaking directly with his staff
The ground was covered with tears of remorse
 For the oak cried out, "God you are the one true source"
The energy shifted and love poured from the oak onto
the ground
Sprouting from the ruins, life was found
Now the two have grown into one
For we can heal only when Gods will is done

Cries of the world

Oh the cries of the world
Oh the cries of life we consider death
When will division stop
When will we look inside
To stare in the mirror at our reflection is not enough
When will we look within and see the light
Do we believe the light is still burning anymore

Oh the cries of the world
Oh the cries of the innocent we say are guilty and
wrong
Why do we continue to choose sides, good vs evil
Why do we say we want peace but only separate
ourselves
Do we want to punish ourselves
Do we not have the faith to believe peace is possible
anymore

Oh the cries of the world
Oh the cries of life's unanswered questions
Will we submit and believe in the unknowing known of
God again
Is it our nature that we will always be lost until we
search for God

Are we only focusing on the path and not the
destination
We chatter daily about how the world is so sad yet we
make up the world
When will we realize the cries of the world are Gods
cries
Oh the cries of God

The girl who always looked up

To the girl who always looked up

The world wants to know:
What are you looking at?
What do you see up there?
Why do you spend so much time up there?
Do you miss looking down?
Why aren't you looking in the mirror?

I see so much more than the eyes could imagine
I see:
Simplicity in the clouds
Uniqueness in the stars
Life in the air
Love in the rain
Miracles in the rainbows
My reflection in creation

I choose to glance down to see the divineness that exists
below

Now the world asks me:
Am I able to look up?

How can I look up?
Who can join me in the clouds?
What exists in my unknown?
Does creation ever stop evolving?
What does the universe want me to see with my own
eyes?

You'll find your answers when you look up

Look up to God to show your smile

Resistance is beautiful

Resistance is the refusal to comply
Refusal to comply with the worlds views of genocide
It is the measure of opposition to the current flow in an
electrical circuit
Lies that are told in our world are so deliberate
Lets analyze this formula $R = V/I$
Come on we can do better, we can try
Resistance is an independent variable standing on its
own
But when he waves the flag high, he is not alone
There is no outside variable that can affect or change its
outcome
But shouldn't we be scared to become forever numb
Resistance depends on the material; cross sectional area
and length
Therefore as the occupation length increases, the
magnitude of resistance leads only to strength
The factors which create resistance are internal, part of,
or as from one source
The very soul of life only takes one course
Resistance is represented by the omega symbol
Explain to me why the world is so sinful
As the last letter of the Greek alphabet
I say with all resistance it is set

"I am the alpha and the omega, the first and the last, the beginning and the end"
In this world resistance is beautiful beyond what we can comprehend

The man-made forest

Yell at the world
Scream and let pain escape
Let anguish release the burden of souls
Lament the ways of the world
Burn materialism to free the mind
But beware and become aware
Words will fall where pollen lands
Look around and realize your surroundings
The leaves under your feet are crushed by your weight
The sky above you is still and humbly waiting
To scream in a man made forest is a cry attempting to
reach the depths of the ocean
Fall silent and God will change your cries into prayers
You will never again yell in a man made forest

Let the world change you

They said don't let the world change you but it did
They told you don't let the world change you but that's
all they said
Words they told you to follow blindly
Words from religious text but not spoken from the heart
of God

They said don't let the world harden your heart but it
did
Your heart closed to evil and opened to love
It strengthened its very muscle fibers with the power of
authenticity

They said don't let the world change you but it did
The world blinded you with evil acts and made you turn
around
It made you look at past hatred and the wheel of power
still turning

They said don't let the world change you but it did
The world showed you the skeleton left of humanity
It made you honor the martyr of death which gave new
life

They said don't let the world change you
They said you can't change the world as one being
They said if you focus on the world you lose perspective

They said don't let the world change you but it did
Seeing the world with open eyes made you grieve
This deep grief is your great act of love for the world

They said don't let the world change you
But I say let the world change you

Coinciding hearts

Across the world but together in soul
You say beautiful hearts coincide
And we both know this world is a lie
My eyes see your heart
Your heart sees my eyes
When we are one, we become the body of God
My eternity thanks you for what you have given me
A universal gift to be shared with the world

21st century holocaust

Imagine the world advancing exponentially through
technology, space and science
But then within that world the only stagnant energy is
humans
We are able to be spies and watch the life of anyone we
choose
We stare at screens to try to make us feel alive
We listen to music to feel emotions
We watch horror unfold and then wonder why more
people didn't stop the holocaust when it was happening
I am starting to see that while the external factors of life
whirled past us, we never blinked
But are we really still stuck staring at another holocaust
not moving or have we become robots who aren't
programmed to see
What if it took a letter to someone living in a 21st
century holocaust to make us open our eyes
This letter though is now morphed into online messaging
through social media
What do you say to someone who you are watching
being starved, bombed and their families displaced
What would you actually say to a holocaust victim on
your "live feed"
Can your privilege save them or would you have to shut

down as you realize your privilege is their oppression
Why is comfort our off switch as humans
Can we even still say honestly that human suffering can
evoke change in us when we can't control our own
design
Is the only part of us still functioning the shell of a body
which eats and breathes
Meanwhile the holocaust victim is the only evolving
human left
They hold the key to our humanity
They are a light that is so powerful it will reboot all of
humanity who chose to look at it
They continue to share love despite being stripped of
their bodies
When you wonder what it would be like to write a letter
to a holocaust victim blink because you have unread
messages

Healing and hope

What a slippery slope
One soul interlocks with another
Carrying the weak through to summer
A seed of joy planted
As every desire will be granted
The gardener now in admiration
For healing and hope have changed the new generation

A lifestyle of learning

Starts with sunlight
Quickly you soar to new heights
Perspectives change
Elevation makes it hard for you to expand
You wish to slow down but you see it is planned
The spark you crave to uncover
Made you a wild book lover
Curiosity is your vehicle
For now you learned the pinnacle
Your souls joy is this yearning

Anniversary

How do I say "happy" anniversary in our circumstance
How do I recall beautiful times while we struggle to
survive
My memory is gone, lost in this moment
But if I am to be lost, let me escape with you
My dear, my heart, the eyes to my life
Life continues with you
Our memories are held precious with God
Awaiting us like the treasure of our future
I will search my soul and share the last piece of me with
you
I tell you my love, this life will never compare
What we have in this moment is ours to bear

Red haired girl

In a world full of blondes and brunettes there stood a girl
with red hair
She yelled for truth and justice
Only to be met by the worlds blank stare
She wondered how could nobody care
Would they if they truly saw
Or was the burden of sin replicated in our DNA too
much to bare
Still she continued to dare
Pushing the envelope until she could no longer
She fell to her knees in despair
She crawled along her path alone
Sorting in her mind how this world could be so unfair
Grappling with the idea peace could be as thin as the air
She still wanted to share
Her voice was powerful and her prayers echoed
Could she be the key to start the repair
If each soul could become aware
Would we find love is not so rare

Palestinian smile

To see a Palestinian smile
Resisting through the Nakba to the Palestinian
Holocaust
Some might say it spans from the river to the sea
So wide so deep, it's a love we might not have seen
It shines through the darkness and hold reverence to the
past
But this smile, Palestine will always last

A new day

You cry in the rain, you teeter on the edge, you wait in the silence, you sit in the pain
You stay stuck so long you cramp in this position and anguish from the mental strain
You know there is a way and there is a light, you see it outside through the sun rays and birds basking in the bird bath
Then comes a fresh hello, an idiosyncratic laugh, a message from your past, here comes your new path
Excitement ignites as this fresh friendship begins
You sync so effortlessly, you question if your souls are twins
She did the work, she opened the window. All to let the gust of life's wind reinvigorate your being
This shared portal of life, now you both are seeing

Affirmations

In Gods arms we are one
In Gods arms we are released
In Gods arms we share souls
In Gods arms we can see
In Gods arms we are created

Sparks

Your soul cannot see without light
Do not attempt to smother your spark with a blanket,
hiding it away from life
Joy is shown through another's smile so bright
For all of existence is shared like husband and wife

Simple pleasures delighted
Tea candles flickering from your bathtub views
Its as if your manifestations have been sighted
With momentum built and desires fired, now is your
time to choose

Will you release the pressure on your bottled sunshine
To illuminate the path that lies before others
The oceans vibration carrying the moon serves as a sign
All light returns home, as children rejoin with their
mothers

Mirrors have shattered, source has spoken, you are the
key and this is your fate
Let the light within you radiate

White love

Is it white love or a white lie?
What is the white American dream
Is it a white picket fence built on a fairy tale of white lies
I'm sorry I meant to say white skies
Or does the sky only look white to "others" as white
phosphorus fills their lungs
Shhh don't say that! Its a lie
Go turn on the white noise, its on channel 13 then go to
work
Remember you worked hard for this white American
dream
Go to work, make money, spend money, desire more
money, give to myself, take from others
Wait... take from others?
Starting to question the innocence they told you of the
white lie
Shhh now is not the place! And remember, it's a lie
You must be lost or worse worshiping the wrong white
God
Put on your white pearls and take yourself down to the
little white church
They surely believe in the good and in the white light
You find your white knight and create a bundle of your
own white love

Your consciousness no longer nags at you as the white
walls of your home deafen you
But one day you are white as a ghost as someone stole
your white bundle of hope
You want to give up and wave your white flag with all
you have left
Shhh... you just want to go back to the white noise
Your void became a magnet for others who have
suffered
White lightning struck and your white eyes closed and
reopened
Your gated community opened up to the world
You see there was never any such thing as white love
This little white lie cost you your white love, all to serve
the white man who isn't above

New leaf

What have you learned
What thoughts need to be burned
Did you turn a new leaf
How will you share your new beliefs
The tides have shifted, the world has turned
Hold high the light your soul has affirmed

My friend is a candle

My friend is a candle
She brings me warmth through her glow
I sit with her and sip on rose tea
She teaches me the value of ease and flow
Here in this moment I can be
We stay motionless, emotions released
For what an experience to be received

Tide

I look down at my feet wading in the shallow tide
The tide comes and goes but I remain planted
How still I am, letting only the ocean foam brush my
ankles. I sink a little deeper into the sand.
I raise my head to see a sun that disappears as the sky
and water become one
Still I remain and the tide comes and goes
My mind evaporates and I am left connecting to all that I
love
I see each smile in Palestine changing the current
I feel the strength of humanity building each wave
higher
I hold my breath experiencing the weight of the
Palestinian suffering crash into me
And then in a moment the tide leaves calmly
The tide woke me up, the tide changed the world
Even if it all dries up, I'll always know; the tide took me
to Palestine where I discovered we were always one